Ancient
GREECE

THE BRITISH MUSEUM
A BOOK OF POSTCARDS

Pomegranate

SAN FRANCISCO

Pomegranate Communications, Inc.
Box 808022, Petaluma, California 94975
800-227-1428
www.pomegranate.com

Pomegranate Europe Ltd.
Unit 1, Heathcote Business Centre
Hurlbutt Road, Warwick, Warwickshire CV34 6TD, U.K.

ISBN 0-7649-2462-1
Pomegranate Catalog No. AA199

Pomegranate publishes books of
postcards on a wide range of subjects.
Please contact the publisher for more information.

Cover designed by Lisa Alban
Printed in China
12 11 10 09 08 07 06 05 04 03   10 9 8 7 6 5 4 3 2 1

To facilitate detachment of the postcards from this book, fold each card along its perforation line before tearing.

Within the collections of the Department of Greek and Roman Antiquities in The British Museum, you will find objects dating back to the beginning of the Bronze Age. This period (c. 3200 B.C.–1100 B.C.) saw the rise of several influential Aegean and eastern Mediterranean cultures and the gradual homogenization of these cultures into what we now regard as ancient Greek civilization. The Minoans on the island of Crete, known for their great palaces resembling town centers, emerged as a regional power, followed by the Mycenaeans, who inhabited the Greek mainland and were the first documented speakers of Greek. Examples of both Minoan and Mycenaean artistry are included here.

After the fall of the Mycenaeans and an ensuing "Dark Age," Greek culture rebounded as it came under the growing influence of Eastern civilizations such as Phoenicia and Egypt. During the Archaic period (c. 600–480 B.C.), Athenian artists perfected the black-figure technique of vase painting and developed a new style of red-figure work. Advances in sculpture and architecture led to the construction of the first large-scale Greek temple, the sanctuary of Artemis at Ephesos in Asia Minor. On the mainland, the four great Panhellenic sanctuaries—at Olympia, Delphi, Isthmia, and Nemea—regularly hosted games as part of religious festivities, which helped to forge a common identity among Greeks from the various city-states.

Greek intellectual and artistic achievements culminated in the Classical period (480–300 B.C.). Many of Greece's greatest poets and thinkers—Pindar, Aeschylus,

Sophokles, Euripides, Socrates, Plato, Aristotle—lived during this time. Also dating from this era are the Parthenon and other famous structures on the Acropolis, products of the architectural revitalization program instituted by the Athenian politician Perikles. The objects featured in this book of postcards include fragments of sculptural decoration and freestanding figures from several Greek monuments; despite the damage they have suffered, these pieces convey the timeless, refined beauty that characterizes Greek sculpture of this period. Oddly enough, this cultural renaissance took place against a backdrop of war—both among the various city-states and between Greek confederates and the encroaching Persians.

Greece did eventually succumb to foreigners—not the Persians, but the Macedonians, led by Philip II. His son, Alexander the Great (356–323 B.C.), continued the program of territorial expansion that Philip left unfinished. With the largest force ever assembled on Greek soil, Alexander—who saw himself as a champion of Greek ideals and the liberator of Greeks from Asiatic rule—set out to conquer the Persian empire. By the time of his death, he ruled most of the known world. During the following Hellenistic period (323–30 B.C.), Greek influence continued to be wide-spread, even as Alexander's empire began to disintegrate. Finally, the glory days of ancient Greece came to a close as the next great power marched onto the world stage—Rome.

Ancient GREECE

Bronze group of a bull and an acrobat
Minoan, c. 1700–1450 B.C.
From island of Crete
L: 15.5 cm; H: 11.4 cm
Spencer Churchill Collection
The British Museum GR 1966.3-28.1

BOX 808022   PETALUMA   CA 94975

Pomegranate

Ancient GREECE
Bronze griffin head
Greek, Orientalizing period, c. 650 B.C.
Probably made on island of Rhodes
H: 23.4 cm; W: 2.7 cm; Wt: 265 g
The British Museum GR 1870.3-15.16

BOX 808022   PETALUMA   CA 94975

Pomegranate

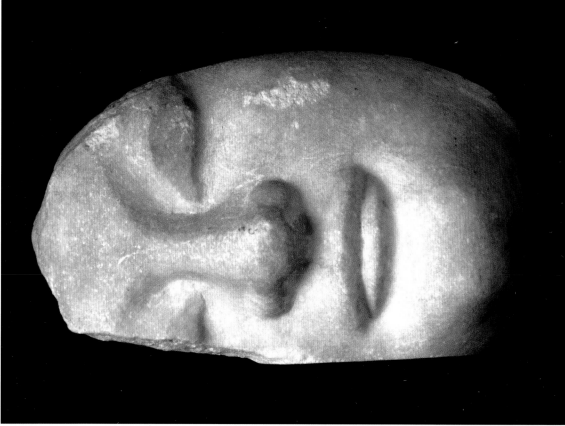

Ancient GREECE

Marble head of a woman
Greek, c. 550–520 B.C.
From the Temple of Artemis at Ephesos, modern Turkey
H: 19 cm
Excavated by John Turtle Wood
The British Museum GR 1873.5-5.43

BOX 808022   PETALUMA   CA 94975

Pomegranate

Ancient GREECE

Bronze figure of a running girl
Greek, c. 520–500 B.C.
Found at Prizren, Serbia; possibly made in or near Sparta, Greece
H: 11.4 cm
The British Museum GR 1876.5-10.1

BOX 808022 PETALUMA CA 94975

Pomegranate

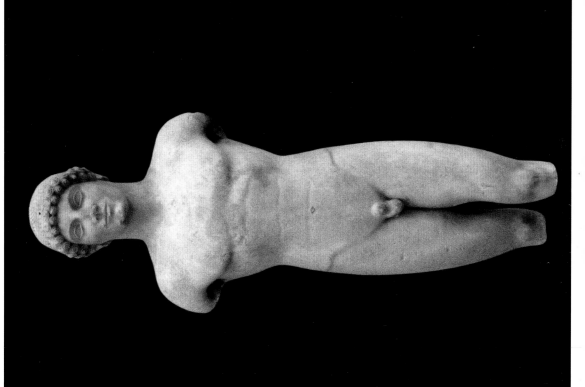

Ancient GREECE

The Strangford Apollo
Greek, c. 500–490 B.C.
Allegedly from island of Anáfi, Cyclades
H: 101 cm
Strangford Collection
The British Museum GR 1864.2-20.1

BOX 808022 PETALUMA CA 94975

Pomegranate

Ancient GREECE

Red-figured cup, attrib. to the Brygos Painter
Greek, c. 490–480 B.C.
Made in Athens, Greece; found at Vulci, Etruria (now Lazio, Italy)
H: 12.7 cm; D: 32 cm
The British Museum GR 1848.6-19.7

BOX 808022   PETALUMA   CA 94975

Pomegranate

Ancient GREECE

Silver *tetradrachm* of Athens
Greek, c. 480 B.C.
From Athens, Greece
D: 22 mm; Wt: 16.64 g
Gift of Dr. F. Parkes Weber
The British Museum CM 1906-11-3-2591

BOX 808022   PETALUMA   CA 94975

Pomegranate

Ancient GREECE
Terracotta relief showing Skylla
Greek, c. 465–435 B.C.
From island of Mílos; found on island of Aegina
H: 12.5 cm
The British Museum GR 1867.5-8.673

BOX 808022   PETALUMA   CA 94975

Pomegranate

Ancient GREECE

Marble metope from the Parthenon
The Acropolis, Athens, Greece, c. 440 B.C.
H: 172 cm
Elgin Collection
The British Museum GR South Metope XXVII

BOX 808022 PETALUMA CA 94975

Pomegranate

Pomegranate

BOX 808022   PETALUMA   CA 94975

Ancient GREECE

Silver *tetradrachm* of Demetrius Poliorcetes
Macedonian, 301–283 B.C.
From the mint of Salamis, island of Cyprus
D: 26 mm
The British Museum CM 1873-8-3-1

Pomegranate

BOX 808022   PETALUMA   CA 94975

Pomegranate

BOX 808022   PETALUMA   CA 94975

Ancient GREECE

Bronze statuette of a huntsman, perhaps Alexander the Great
Hellenistic, c. 250–100 B.C.
H: 47.5 cm
The British Museum GR 1865.5-20.65

Pomegranate

BOX 808022   PETALUMA   CA 94975

Ancient GREECE

Bronze mask of Dionysus
Greco-Roman, c. 200 B.C.–A.D. 100
From Greece
H: 21.4 cm

Purchased with the assistance of the National Heritage Memorial Fund
The British Museum GR 1989.1-30.1

Pomegranate

BOX 808022   PETALUMA   CA 94975

Ancient GREECE

Portrait statuette of Socrates
Greek, c. 200 B.C.–A.D. 100
Allegedly from Alexandria, Egypt
H: 27.5 cm
Purchased with the assistance of the National Art Collections Fund
The British Museum GR 1925.11-18.1